Surprised by Subtraction

Book Two of
The Gift of Numbers
Math Fantasy Curriculum

Rachel Rogers and Joe Lineberry

Illustrations by Morgan Swofford

PROSPECTIVE PRESS ACADEMICS

an imprint of
PROSPECTIVE PRESS LLC
1959 Peace Haven Rd, #246, Winston-Salem, NC 27106 U.S.A.
www.prospectivepress.com

Published in the United States of America by PROSPECTIVE PRESS LLC

SURPRISED BY SUBTRACTION

Text copyright © Rachel Rogers and Joe Lineberry, 2017
All rights reserved.
The authors' moral rights have been asserted.

Illustrations © Morgan Swofford, 2017
All rights reserved.
The illustrator's moral rights have been asserted.

Library of Congress Control Number: 2017934693

ISBN 978-1-943419-46-3

Surprised by Subtraction is the second volume in the Gift of Numbers math fantasy curriculum. For information on additional volumes in the series or for bulk sales, please send inquiries to education@prospectivepress.com

Printed in the United States of America
First trade paperback printing August, 2017

1 3 5 7 9 10 8 6 4 2

The text of this book is typeset in Mouse Memoirs
Accent text is typeset in Galindo

PUBLISHER'S NOTE

This book is a work of creative non-fiction with fictional fantasy elements. The people, names, characters, locations, activities, and events portrayed or implied by this book are the product of the author's imagination or are used fictitiously. Any resemblance to actual people, locations, and events is strictly coincidental. Lots of actual exercise was done by the authors before, during, and after the writing of this book.

Without limiting the rights as reserved in the above copyright, no part of this publication may be reproduced, stored in or introduced into any retrieval system, or transmitted–by any means, in any form, electronic, mechanical, photocopying, recording, or otherwise–without the prior written permission of the publisher. Not only is such reproduction illegal and punishable by law, but it also hurts the authors and illustrator who toiled hard on the creation of this work and the publisher who brought it to the world. In the spirit of fair play, and to honor the labor and creativity of the authors and illustrator, we ask that you purchase only authorized electronic and print editions of this work and refrain from participating in or encouraging piracy or electronic piracy of copyright-protected materials. Please give creators a break and don't steal this or any other work.

Dedicated to our loving life partners— Randy and Beth.

Life was better in Odd Nation and Even Land. The even numbers and odd numbers were working together. They were using addition to make more numbers for future girls and boys.

Doctor Even and Doctor Odd were working in the same lab at More Children's Hospital. The dividing wall at the hospital had been torn down. Even numbers and odd numbers could come and go in all sections of the hospital.

King Less was happy and sad. He was happy they were now making more odd and even numbers. Yet he was also sad. He had a feeling that the future girls and boys would need more than just new numbers. He thought to himself, "I need a dream, like King More had. Then I would know what to do."

Days passed and no dream came to King Less. He decided to take a walk. The exercise must have helped, because he came up with a new idea.

"Everyone wants to add more and more," he said to himself. "What if a child wants less? She may want to find the **difference** between two numbers. She can't just add the two numbers together."

"I predict a time when a girl, named Tonya, will want to have a jumping contest with her younger brother. She wants to see how much farther she can jump than he can. Tonya uses a yardstick and measures her jump—31 inches. She marks a red 'X' on her yardstick at 31 inches—the length of her jump."

"Then Tonya measures her brother's jump—13 inches. She marks a blue 'X' on her yardstick at 13 inches—the length of her brother's jump. She carefully counts the inches between the red 'X' and the blue 'X.' That is the difference in the lengths of their jumps—18 inches.

"Tonya jumped 18 inches farther than her brother."

King Less jumped and shouted, "Counting works, but it takes too much time. We need a new math operation to solve these problems quickly!"

Doctor Odd heard the shouting coming from outside his lab. He ran to a window to find out what was going on. The doctors agreed to search for a new math operation.

After working for a few hours, Doctor Odd and Doctor Even discovered a new math operation called **subtraction**.

Doctor Odd explained to King Less, "Tonya will make an equation. She can start with the bigger number, her jump of 31 inches. Then, she will subtract her brother's jump of 13 inches."

5 SUBTRACTION USING A NUMBER LINE

"Tonya knows her brother's jump of 13 inches is 1 ten and 3 ones. So she subtracts 10 one time, going back on the number line from 31 to 21.

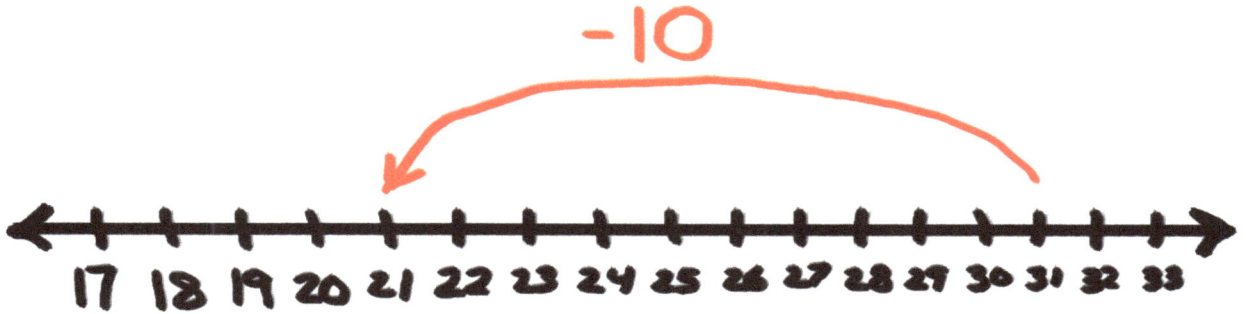

"Tonya has 3 ones left. She subtracts 1 three times from 21 to get 18 as her answer.

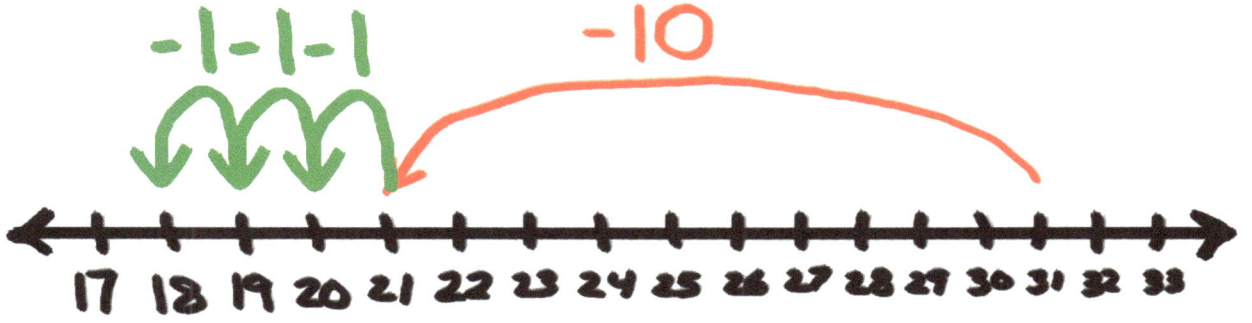

SUBTRACTION USING

"Tonya can use a different strategy. She uses **expanded form** to solve her subtraction problem.

		Tens		Ones
31	=	30	+	1
−13	=	10	+	3

"She looks at the ones place, but she can't subtract 3 ones from 1 one.

EXPANDED FORM

"Tonya trades 1 ten for 10 ones.

		Tens		Ones		Tens		Ones	
31	=	30	+	1	=	20	+	(10 + 1)	11
−13	=	10	+	3	=	10	+	3	

"Now she can subtract 3 ones from 11 ones.

Tens		Ones		
20	+	(10 + 1)		11
10	+	3		
10	+	8	=	18

"Tonya sees that her answer is 18. She jumped 18 inches farther than her brother."

"Wow!" exclaimed King Less. "This subtraction operation is awesome!"

News spread quickly throughout Even Land and Odd Nation. The numbers were now volunteering for addition and subtraction operations at the hospital.

$$8 + 1 = 9$$
$$8 - 1 = 7$$

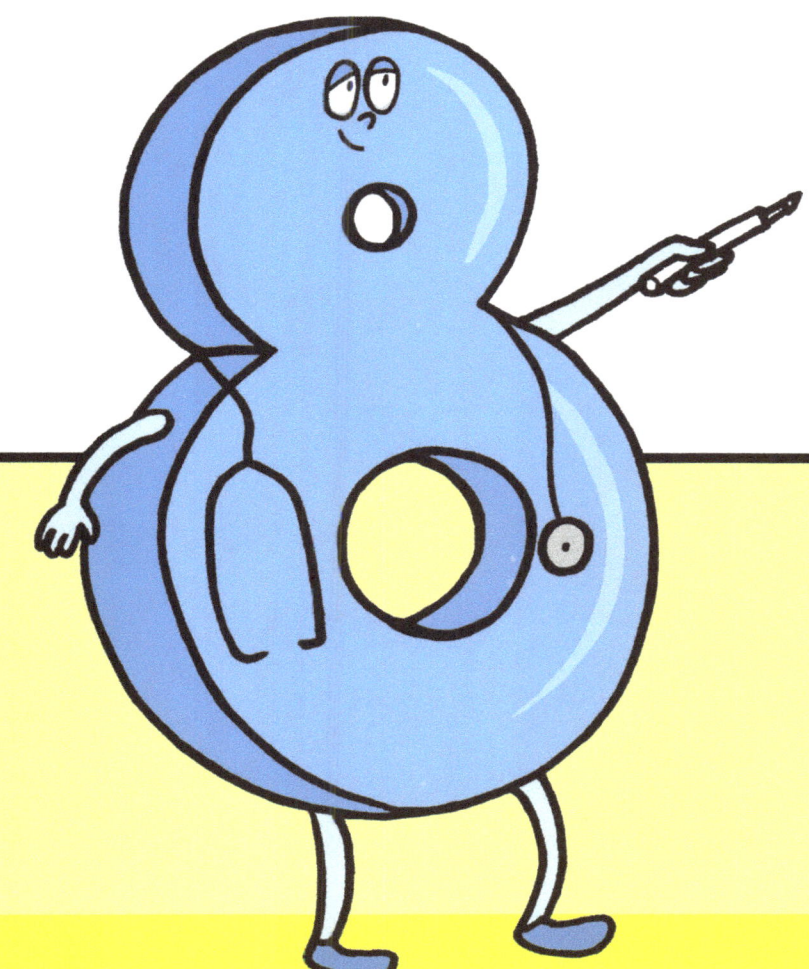

Just like addition, subtraction created more numbers. Unlike addition, subtraction created smaller numbers, not larger numbers.

For example, $8 + 1 = 9$, while $8 - 1 = 7$. The sum of $8 + 1$ is greater than the difference of $8 - 1$.

Subtraction had become a new member of the Operation Club!

Number 6 had come to the hospital to congratulate Doctor Odd and Doctor Even on their discovery. Doctor Odd greeted number 6, "So good to see you, number 6. We have been doing subtraction operations all day. I am so tired, but not too tired to try a new idea. Do you have any new ideas?"

"Well I have been thinking," said number 6. "What happens if you subtract the same number from itself? Like…"

8 − 8 = ☐

"What would that equal?"
"We haven't tried that before. Let's try it," said Doctor Odd.

8 − 8 = 0

The group was surprised. It was the first time they had created number 0. The number 0 looked unusual, like a ghost. He looked like nothing was there. Doctor Odd then tried another new idea. He added number 0 to number 6, and the sum was 6.

$$6 + 0 = 6 \text{ and } 0 + 6 = 6$$

Then the doctor subtracted 0 from number 6. They were all surprised again, because the difference was also 6.

$$6 - 0 = 6$$

King Less had been taking notes. He noticed, "Number 0 is unique. You can add 0 to any number or subtract 0 from any number, and you still get the same number."

"It makes sense to me," said King More. "Number 0 is nothing. If you add nothing to a number, you should get the same number. If you subtract nothing from a number, you should get the same number. This is so fascinating. We have discovered new math facts!"

Suddenly, they heard Doctor Even screaming from a nearby operation room.

They rushed down the hall. A frustrated Doctor Even was looking all around the room, like he had lost something.

Doctor Even cried out, "We can't find number 4. We were adding 3 + 4 to make a new number 7. Here is number 3 and number 7, but number 4 is missing. We can't find him anywhere!"

Everyone was surprised. No number had disappeared before. King Less glared at number 0 and shouted, "I think ghostly zero did this. He is so different. We didn't have this problem until he showed up."

King More tried to calm the group, "We don't know if King Less's idea is true. We have no proof. Let's not blame number zero. Instead, let's think about a solution to this problem."

Doctor Odd thought for a moment and suggested, "What if we use subtraction?"

Doctor Even agreed, "Yes! Let's subtract number 3 from number 7. That should bring back number 4."

$$7 - 3 = 4$$

The idea worked. Number 4 appeared again. The whole group was relieved. Plus, they had some new math facts.

$3 + 4 = 7$

$4 + 3 = 7$

$7 - 4 = 3$

$7 - 3 = 4$

Numbers 3, 4, and 7 became a **fact family!**

If any number ever disappeared, the missing number could be created again using the other numbers in the fact family in an equation.

3 + ☐ = 7, so the missing number is 4.

7 − ☐ = 4, so the missing number is 3.

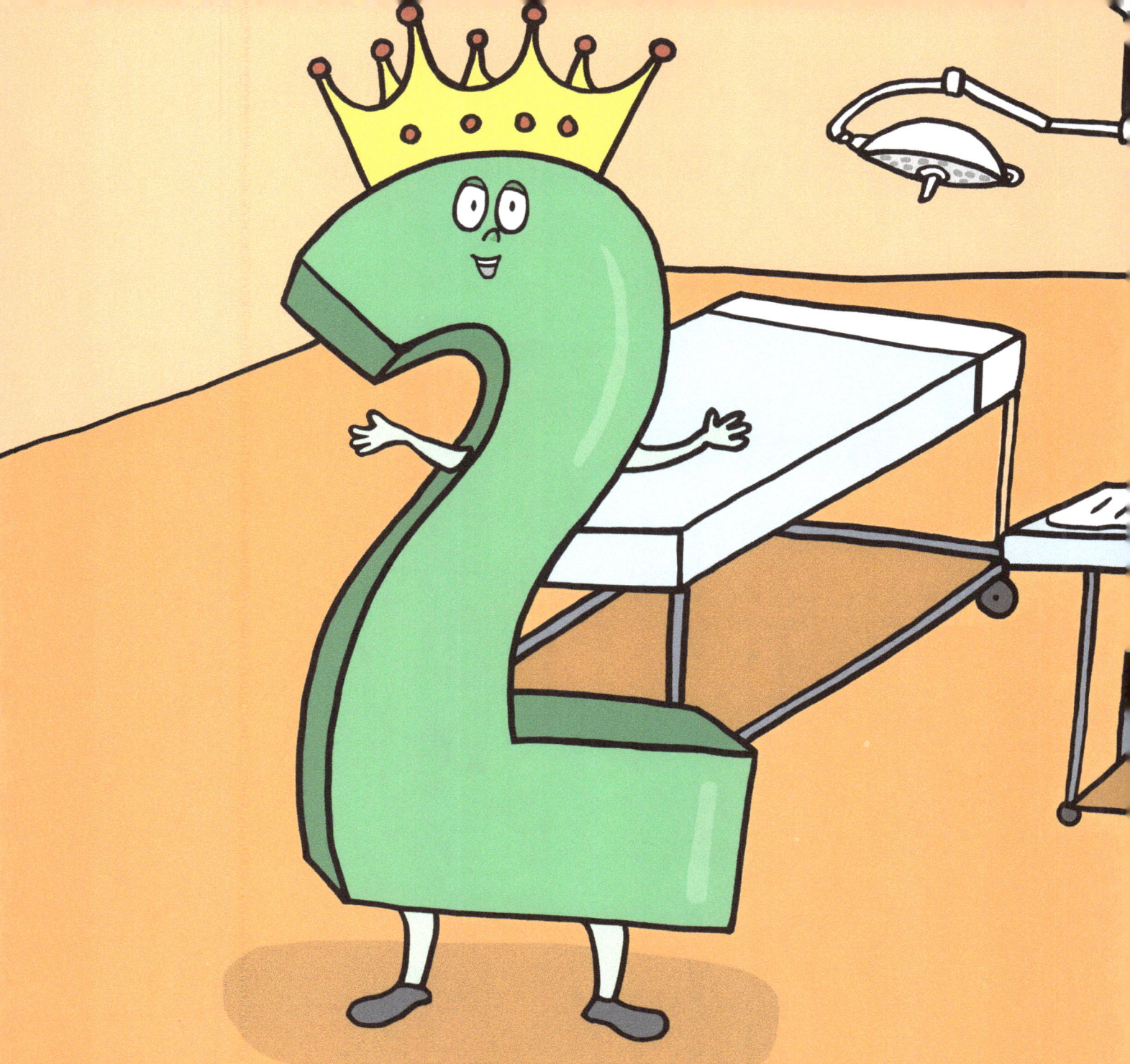

King More had another idea. "Why don't we have the numbers in each fact family live together? If numbers 3, 4, and 7 live together, we don't need to worry about numbers disappearing. We will always be able to create a missing number using his fact family."

By living together, odd and even numbers learned another way to cooperate with each other.

Living in fact families solved the problem of disappearing numbers. With fact families, they could always replace a missing number.

King More and King Less have created fact families. If a number disappears, they want the equations ready to find the missing number. Use the three numbers on the roof to fill in the blanks inside each house. You will make four different equations.

A number disappeared from each family. Help King More and King Less by filling in the missing number on the roof of each house. Inside the house, write the equations that make up each fact family.

Discussion Questions

1. King More got his new idea of addition in a dream, and King Less got his new idea of subtraction after exercising. How do you get your new ideas?

2. Why did King More want the odd and even numbers to live in fact families?

3. What is the author's purpose for writing *Surprised by Subtraction*?

4. Explain (make it clear) what you have learned about subtraction.

5. Compare and contrast (alike/different) addition and subtraction, using the Venn diagram below.

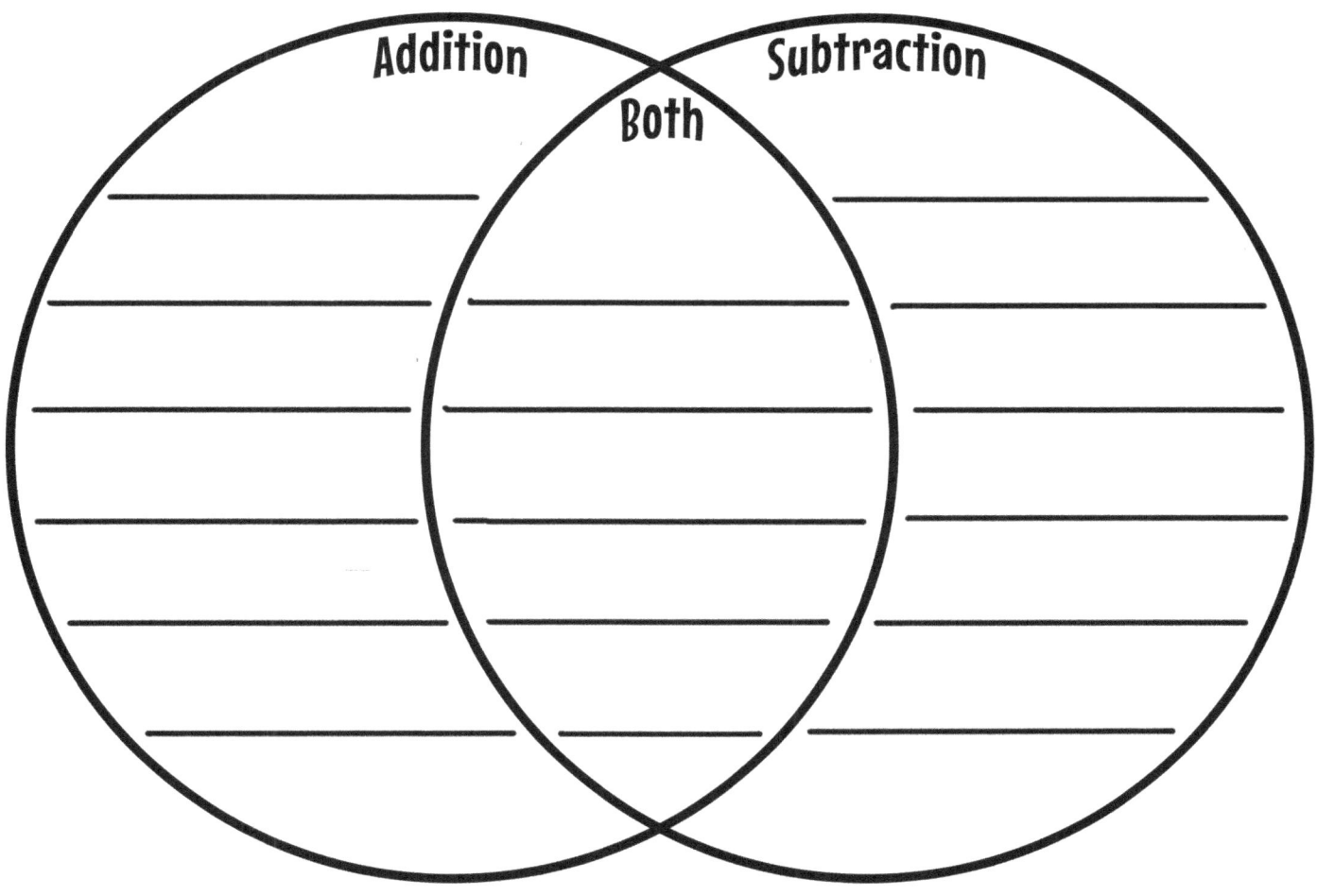

The Publisher hereby grants permission to the original purchaser and/or sole owner of this book to make copies of this page for in-class use only. Copies may not be transmitted, sold, lent, or stored—electronically or otherwise.

Venn Diagram Answer Key

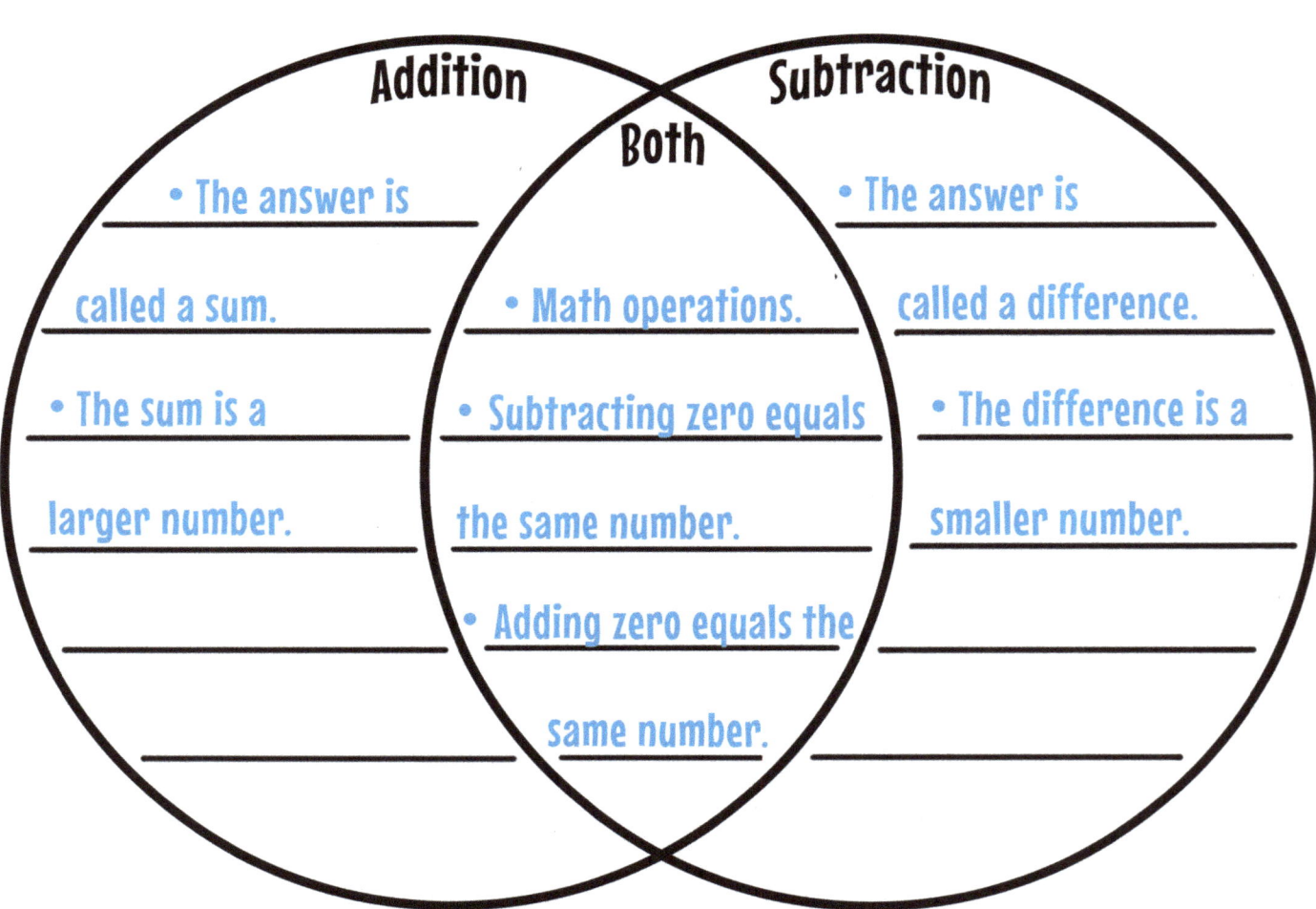

Addition
- The answer is called a sum.
- The sum is a larger number.

Both
- Math operations.
- Subtracting zero equals the same number.
- Adding zero equals the same number.

Subtraction
- The answer is called a difference.
- The difference is a smaller number.

About the Authors

Rachel Rogers
is a 2nd grade teacher at Old Richmond Elementary School, Winston-Salem, NC. She has more than 35 years of experience teaching first, second, and third graders.

Joe Lineberry
told similar stories to his sons when they were growing up. He is also the author of *Let's Stop Playing Games: Finding Freedom in Authentic Living*.

About the Books

The Gift of Numbers
is a math fantasy curriculum that combines literature and mathmatics in a fun, age-appropriate series for second- and third-grade students.

- Volume 1: *Saved by Addition*
- Volume 2: *Surprised by Subtraction*
- Volume 3: *Graphing the Mystery*
- Volume 4: *Adventure with Fractions*
- Volume 5: *Multiplication Football*
- Volume 6: *The Experiment Game*
- Volume 7: *Division Gymnastics*

www.ingramcontent.com/pod-product-compliance
Lightning Source LLC
Chambersburg PA
CBHW051254110526
44588CB00026B/2996